KINGFISHER
LONDON & NEW YORK

KINGFISHER
LONDON & NEW YORK

Text and illustration copyright © Macmillan Publishers International Ltd 2025
First published in 2025 in the United States by Kingfisher
120 Broadway, New York, NY 10271
Kingfisher is an imprint of
Macmillan Children's Books, London

Distributed in the U.S. and Canada by Macmillan,
120 Broadway, New York, NY 10271

Library of Congress Cataloging-in-Publication Data has been applied for

ISBN 978-0-7534-8122-6

Kingfisher books are available for special promotions and premiums.
For details contact: Special Markets Department, Macmillan,
120 Broadway, New York, NY 10271

For more information, please visit
www.kingfisherbooks.com

Printed in China
2 4 6 8 9 7 5 3 1

EU representative: 1st Floor, The Liffey Trust Centre,
117-126 Sheriff Street Upper, Dublin 1 D01 YC43

FSC
www.fsc.org

MIX
Paper | Supporting
responsible forestry
FSC® C116313

Let's Meet
MESSI

ILLUSTRATED BY GERALDINE RODRÍGUEZ
WRITTEN BY CATHERINE SAUNDERS

On June 24, 1987, in Rosario, a city in Argentina,
Jorge Messi and Celia Cuccittini celebrated
the birth of their new baby boy.

They named him Lionel, which means
"young lion"—or Leo, for short.

Leo had two big brothers who loved playing
soccer on the streets near their house.

As soon as he could
walk, Leo joined in.
Although he was the
smallest, Leo was
soon the best player!

Leo was happiest when he was playing soccer.
He was really fast and scored a lot of goals,
usually with his left foot.

His brothers called him
"la pulgita," which
means "little flea" in
Spanish, because he
was small and strong.

At the age of four, Leo joined his very first team, Grandoli. His grandmother often took him to games and watched him play.

LEO! LEO!

She was his biggest fan, and Leo loved to make her feel proud.

When Leo started school, he played soccer during all his breaks. Everyone wanted to be on his team because it meant that they would probably win the game!

Leo dreamed of being a professional soccer player when he grew up. When he was just six years old, his local team, Newell's Old Boys, asked him to play for their youth team.

Leo was fairly shy, but playing soccer made him feel confident.
In his first game for Newell's Old Boys, he scored four goals.

His team didn't lose a game for three years!

When he was about 10 years old, doctors told Leo that he needed some special expensive medicine to help his body grow.

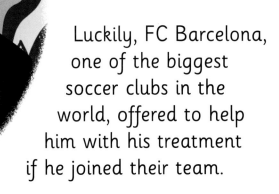

Luckily, FC Barcelona, one of the biggest soccer clubs in the world, offered to help him with his treatment if he joined their team.

So Leo moved thousands of miles away to Spain, where he joined FC Barcelona's youth training academy.

He lived there with his dad, but his mom, brothers, and little sister stayed in Argentina.

Leo missed the rest of his family, but he made a lot of friends at the FC Barcelona training academy, La Masia.

When they weren't playing soccer, they liked to play video games together . . . about soccer!

At just 16 years old, Leo played his first game for Barcelona's main team. His dream of becoming a professional soccer player had come true!

He couldn't wait to play with some of the best and most well-known players in the world.

Leo played wonderfully, and soon he was famous all over the world, too.

People loved watching him score incredible goals and help Barcelona win lots of trophies. Leo was even voted the best player on the planet.

He once scored five goals in a single game!

Leo was 18 years old when he began playing for his country, Argentina. Seeing him in the famous blue-and-white shirt made Leo's family so proud.

A few years later, Leo became Argentina's captain. It was a big responsibility, but he was ready to be a leader on the field.

Off the field, Leo was a great friend to his teammates. He was also a superstar soccer player with millions of fans!

But life wasn't all about soccer for Leo. With his wife, Antonela, he had three sons. He loved being a dad even more than he loved playing soccer!

Leo felt very lucky. It made him want to help other people, too.

He set up his own charity, the Leo Messi Foundation, to help children all around the world.

After more than 20 years at FC Barcelona, Leo decided to move to a new team in France, called Paris Saint-Germain, or PSG.

MESSI
30

His Barcelona fans were sad to see him go, but everyone still loved to watch him play soccer.

All around the world, children looked up to Leo.
They tried to copy his ball skills and wore shirts
with his name and number on them.

Although Leo had won many trophies with his clubs, there was still something he hoped to win—a trophy for Argentina!

As captain, Leo had to inspire his team. He encouraged them to try as hard as they could and to never give up.

Finally, Argentina triumphed at the Copa América,
a South American soccer tournament.

Now there was just one more trophy Leo wanted
to win for his country—the World Cup.

Leo had played in four World Cups with Argentina and lost two finals. Although he was heartbroken, he was determined that his fifth World Cup would be different.

Even after Argentina lost their first game,
Leo was still sure they could win.

He inspired his teammates to really believe in themselves . . . and they did it! Leo and his squad became World Cup winners at last!

Now Leo had won more trophies than any other player before him, but he wasn't ready to stop playing soccer yet.

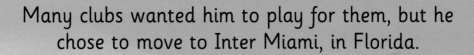

Many clubs wanted him to play for them, but he chose to move to Inter Miami, in Florida.

Leo was keen to share his skills with new fans and to show them why he thinks soccer is the best game in the world.

Leo practices a lot to keep his skills sharp and his body fit and strong. He knows that playing soccer is hard work—but it's worth it!

Leo loves to bring joy to his fans, especially children. He always makes time to sign autographs and pose for photos.

When he's not playing for his team, Leo likes to hang out with his family and friends—and even play some soccer!

Many people think that so far Leo is the greatest soccer player ever. Maybe that's why he's been voted the best player in the world an incredible eight times.

But that's not the most important thing to Leo.
He just loves playing soccer!

When he has the ball at his feet, he still feels like that happy little boy playing on the streets of Rosario.